CONTENTS

1. Introduction to Macbeth.
2. Plot & structure.
3. Character overview.
4. Macbeth.
5. How Macbeth changes.
6. Lady Macbeth.
7. The Witches.
8. King Duncan.
9. Banquo
10. Macduff
11. Overview of themes.
12. The supernatural.
13. Ambition & power.
14. Masculine & feminine
15. Appearance & reality.
16. Guilt & regret.
17. Good & evil.
18. Fear & bravery.
19. Kingship - loyalty & betrayal.
20. Life & death.
21. Form & structure.
22. In the exam.
23. Examples of specific language/literary devices.
24. Examples of specific language/literary devices.
25. Examples of specific language/literary devices.
26. Questions to think about.
27. Notes.

INTRODUCTION TO MACBETH

COMMON THEMES

Shakespeare wrote 38 plays (including 10 tragedies) of which Macbeth is one.

Macbeth includes some of Shakespeare's favourite tragic themes, including...
- AMBITION
- THE SUPERNATURAL
- GOOD & EVIL
- REVENGE
- WHAT IT MEANS TO BE A MAN

SETTING & MOOD

- The MOOD is gloomy with battles, murders, ghosts, witches, talk of evil spirits, mental distress & a suicide.

- The action is split between the elemental chaos of the OUTDOORS (the heath & Birnam Woods) and...

INSIDE THE CASTLE WALLS

where murders are plotted, evil broods & people lose their minds.

The castles include... Dunsinane (Macbeth's), Dunsinane (the King's) & England.

THE REAL MACBETH

Many of the characters in the play, such as Macbeth, King Duncan & his son Prince Malcolm were historical figures that Shakespeare read about, though the story is fictional.

WHO WROTE IT?

William Shakespeare - playwright

Born in 1564 in Stratford upon Avon.

For most of his life he wrote plays for the Lord Chamberlain's Men, which were performed at the Globe Theatre in London.

- Regarded as the greatest writer in the English language, his work is performed more than anyone else's in the world.

CONTEXT

- In Elizabethan times, plays were the most popular form of entertainment. Macbeth was written as a entertainment (1606 - King James I was crowned). As a patron of Shakespeare's work, the then king influenced the content (King James I was very religious & hated witchcraft).

- Hot topics of the time were the dangers of witchcraft, treason & loyalty.

- It is thought to be based on a real historical figure (called Macbeth).

Plot & Structure

Act One

- Macbeth & Banquo returning from battle are met on the heath by three witches. They greet Macbeth as 'Thane of Glamis' (his title). They predict he will be Thane of Cawdor, then King. They predict Banquo's sons will be kings, though he will not, then vanish.
- King Duncan rewards Macbeth with a new title 'Thane of Cawdor' (1st prediction true).
- Macbeth writes a letter explaining events to Lady Macbeth. She immediately plots to murder Duncan. Macbeth procrastinates, but his wife convinces him that they must do it that night, while his guards (drugged) are sleeping.

Act Two

- Macbeth is afraid, but a vision of a dagger leads him to the King's chamber to do the deed. Macbeth returns carrying the bloody daggers. Lady Macbeth returns to the crime scene & plants the weapon on the guards.
- When the murder is discovered (by Macduff & Ross) Macbeth kills the two guards before they can tell the truth. Fearing they will be next, Prince Malcolm & Donalbain flee (Malcolm to England, Donalbain to Ireland) & people speculate they may have been involved.
- Macbeth is crowned King of Scotland (2nd prediction true).

Act Three

- Macbeth remembers the 3rd prediction; 'Banquo's sons will be kings.' He orders Banquo & his son Fleance killed, but Fleance escapes.
- Macbeth sees the bloody ghost of Banquo in his seat at the banquet & behaves so bizarrely that his wife asks the guests to leave.
- Macbeth tells Lady Macbeth he must return to the witches.

Act Four

- Macbeth finds the witches around a cauldron & demands to know the future. The first warns Macbeth to beware of Macduff. The second tells him 'none of woman born shall harm him' & the third informs him that he will not be defeated until 'Birnam woods move.' Though the last two give him confidence, just in case, he orders Macduff to be killed.
- Meanwhile having figured out the truth, Macduff is with Malcolm, planning to retake the crown (with the English troops). Ross arrives & informs Macduff that his wife & family have been killed. Macduff swears revenge.
- Back at the castle, Lady Macbeth is now wandering incoherently with guilt, unable to clean the 'hands of blood' & a doctor is called.

Act Five

- Macbeth prepares the Scottish army to fight after news that Macduff, Malcolm & the English army are waiting to attack at Birnam Wood. Malcolm's army disguise themselves with branches as they approach & when Macbeth is told the wood is moving, he realises the danger he is in.
- Lady Macbeth jumps from the roof & kills herself.
- Hopeful of the final promise that he cannot be killed 'by man of woman born', Macbeth leaves the castle where he is confronted by Macduff. They fight & Macbeth tells Macduff that he cannot harm him, but Macduff reveals he was not born naturally, but by caesarean section, before killing Macbeth & allowing Prince Malcolm to be restored as King.

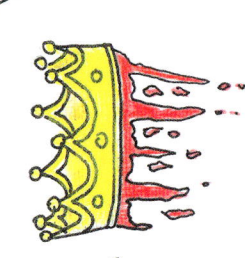

CHARACTER OVERVIEW

THE WITCHES
- Three supernatural figures who huddle on the heath muttering spells & prophecies, which set in motion a series of tragic events which alter Macbeth's life forever.

IMPORTANT MINOR CHARACTERS

HECATE - The goddess of witchcraft who suggests to the witches how to hurt Macbeth further.

GUARDS - Are blamed for the murder of Duncan.

THE MURDERERS - Kill Banquo & Macduff's family for payment.

MACDUFF - A loyal soldier who realises what Macbeth has done. As a result, his family (Lady Macduff & their children) are murdered.

MACBETH
- A brave & loyal soldier (Thane of Glamis) until his ambition is ignited by a prediction & he becomes a ruthless murderer.

LADY MACBETH
- Macbeth's fiercely ambitious wife who calls on evil spirits to help her gain the power she desires. Later, tormented by guilt, she takes her own life.

BANQUO
- Macbeth's close friend, honourable & wise. He remains unchanged by the witches' predictions.

FLEANCE
- Banquo's son. According to the witches, one day will be king. Macbeth tries to have him murdered, but he escapes.

KING DUNCAN
- The noble, fair & trusting King of Scotland.

MALCOLM & DONALBAIN
- The princes/Duncan's sons who flee after their father is killed.

ROSS, LENOX & ANGUS
- Noblemen. They join the rebel team to help Malcolm become king.

ALSO...

DOCTOR & GENTLEWOMAN - Witnesses to Lady Macbeth's ramblings & confession.

OLD MAN - A bystander whose comments might represent the 'common man'.

PORTER - A drunk gatekeeper/comic relief after Duncan's death.

MACBETH

WHO IS HE?
- The **PROTAGONIST**. A loyal general whose ambition (his fatal flaw) is ignited by the witches' predictions.
- Urged on by his wife, he murders the king.
- He stops at nothing to remain as king, but dies in the process.

EARLY ON IN THE PLAY, MACBETH IS DESCRIBED AS HAVING MANY GOOD QUALITIES...

BRAVE — 'For brave Macbeth - well he deserves that name -/Disdaining fortune, with his brandish'd steel,/which smoked with bloody execution.' (Captain 1.2)

GOOD — 'Yet do I fear thy nature;/It is too full o' th' milk of human kindness...' (Lady Macbeth 1.5)

LOVED & ADMIRED — 'We love him highly...' 'O valiant cousin! Worthy gentleman!' (Duncan 1.2)

A FRIEND — 'My noble partner.' (Banquo 1.3)

BUT HE HAS MANY FLAWS...

AMBITIOUS — 'The Prince of Cumberland! That is a step/On which I must fall down, or else o'er-leap,/For in my way it lies. Stars, hide your fires;/Let not light see my black and deep desires.' (Macbeth 1.4)

EASILY LED/MANIPULATED — 'Hie thee hither,/That I may pour my spirits in thine ear,/And chastise with the valour of my tongue.' (Lady Macbeth 1.5)

MORAL — 'Art not without ambition but without/The illness should attend it.' (Lady Macbeth 1.5)

HONOURABLE — 'The Thane of Cawdor lives: why do you dress me/In borrow'd robes?' (Macbeth 1.3)

'There's daggers in men's smiles...'

LACKS DETERMINATION — 'I have no spur/To prick the sides of my intent, but only/Vaulting ambition, which o'erleaps itself/And falls on th'other.' (Macbeth 1.7)

COWARDLY — 'If we fail?' (Macbeth 1.7)

CHANGEABLE — 'We will proceed no further in this business./He hath honour'd me of late..' (Macbeth 1.7)

WRESTLES SELF — 'Who should against his murderer shut the door,/Not bear the knife myself.' (Macbeth 1.7)

How Macbeth Changes

How The Relationship Between The Macbeths Changes

- When Macbeth writes the letter near the beginning of the play it shows AFFECTION & COMMITMENT, 'my dearest partner of greatness'. (1.5)

- They TALK CLOSELY & HONESTLY & he seems KEEN TO PLEASE her with his actions.

- When he hears of her mental health troubles, he appears to NO LONGER CARE.

- At first, Lady Macbeth is OVERBEARING & BOSSY 'Are you a man?' (3.4)

- But when her husband kills more people, she REGRETS HIS RUTHLESS ACTIONS. 'The Thane of Fife had a wife, where is he now?' (5.1)

Courageous
'I have almost forgot the taste of fears. The time has been, my senses would have cool'd to hear a night-shriek…' (Macbeth 3.2)

Possessed
'O, full of scorpions is my mind dear wife! Thou know'st Banquo and his Fleance, lives.' (Macbeth 3.5)

Transparent
'Your face, my thane, is as a book where men / May read strange matters.' (Lady Macbeth 1.5)

'...an untitled tyrant bloody-scepter'd.'

Hysterical
'Methought I heard a voice cry 'sleep no more! Macbeth does murder sleep…' (Macbeth 2.2)

Tortured
'Whose horrid image doth unfix my hair / And make my seated heart knock at my ribs.' (Macbeth 1.3)

Regretful
'Wake Duncan with thy knocking! I would thou couldst!' (Macbeth 2.2)

- The tragic story shows Macbeth's downfall from BRAVE SOLDIER to POWER-HUNGRY MURDERER.

- Because of his FATAL FLAW, he changes from loyal, almost hesitant man to an out of control murderer who will kill anyone who stands in his way of power.

Guided By Evil
'Is this a dagger which I see before me, / The handle towards my hand? Come, let me clutch thee. / I have thee not, and yet I see thee still.' (Macbeth 2.1)

A Murderer
'Hear it not, Duncan, for it is a knell / That summons thee to heaven or to hell.' (Macbeth 2.1)

Guilty
'I am afraid to think what I have done; Look on't again, I dare not.' (Macbeth 2.2)

LADY MACBETH

WHO IS SHE?
- Macbeth's wife, ambitious & manipulative.
- She responds immediately to his letter by calling on evil spirits to help achieve her desire for power (sometimes called the 4th witch).
- Despite her coldness, ultimately her guilt sends her mad & she kills herself.

BUT...

SHE HAS A CONSCIENCE
'Had he not resembled/My father as he slept, I had done't.' (Lady Macbeth 2.2)

SHE HAS HELP
'That which hath made them drunk hath made me bold;'

'Come, thick night,/And pall thee in the dunnest smoke of hell,/That my keen knife see not the wound it makes...' (Lady Macbeth 2.2)

CHARACTER CHANGE?

SHOWS REMORSE
'What's done cannot be undone.' (Lady Macbeth 5.1)

SHE LOSES HER MIND WITH GUILT
(perhaps a victim of the evil she called on) 'What will these hands never be clean?' (Lady Macbeth 5.1)
(Eventually taking her own life)

IN CONTROL
'Leave all the rest to me.' (Lady Macbeth 1.5)

MASCULINE
'Bring forth men-children only;' (Macbeth 2.1)

COLD
'...the dead,/Are but as pictures.' (Lady Macbeth 2.2)

MURDEROUS
'My dearest partner of greatness'

'I would while it was smiling in my face,/Have pluck'd my nipple from his boneless gums,/And dash'd the brains out...' (Lady Macbeth 1.7)

DETERMINED
'But screw your courage to the sticking-place,/And we'll not fail.' (Lady Macbeth 1.7)

AMBITIOUS
'Stop up the...passage to remorse/That no compunctious visitings of nature/shake my fell purpose...' (Lady Macbeth 1.5)

KNOWS HER HUSBAND
'Yet do I fear thy nature;/It is too full o'the milk of human kindness/To catch the nearest way...' (Lady Macbeth 1.5)

MANIPULATIVE
'Hie thee hither,/That I may pour my spirits in thine ear...' (Lady Macbeth 1.5)

AGENT OF EVIL
'Come, you spirits...unsex me here,/And fill me from the crown to the toe top-full/Of direst cruelty!' (Lady Macbeth 1.5)

6

THE WITCHES

COMPELLING & ATTRACTIVE
'Would they had stayed!' (Macbeth 1.3)

VIOLENT
'Where hast thou been sister?/ Killing swine.' (Witches 1.3)

ENJOY DISORDER
'For a charm of powerful trouble,/ Like a hell-broth boil and bubble.' (Witches 1.1)

TALK IN RIDDLES
'Lesser than Macbeth, and greater.'
'...so happy, yet much happier.'
'Thou shalt get kings, though thou be none...' (Witches 1.3)

DECEPTIVE
'Macbeth shall never vanquished be until/ Great Birnam Wood to high Dunsinane Hill shall come against him.' (Witch apparition 4.1)

USE BODY PARTS
'...pilot's thumb...' (Witches 1.3)

OTHER WORLDLY
'...what are these, so wither'd and so wild in their attire,/ That look not like inhabitants o' the earth.' (Banquo 1.3)
'What can the devil speak true?' (Banquo 1.3)

EVIL

CLAIRVOYANT
'All hail Macbeth, thou shalt be King hereafter!' (1.3)

KNOW THEIR OWN
'By the pricking of my thumbs,/ Something wicked this way comes.' (Witches 4.1)

WHO ARE THEY?
- Three mysterious figures huddled round a cauldron, casting spells & discussing Macbeth.
- Their predictions for Macbeth are the catalyst for his actions in the play.
- Ultimately their final prediction & the false confidence it gives, leads to Macbeth's death (killed by Macduff).

HOW THEY CHANGE
Their first prophesies are simple & true, but their latter ones trick Macbeth.

THE WITCHES ARE...

PLAYFUL/FORESHADOWING
'Fair is foul and foul is fair/ Hover through the fog and filthy air.' (Witches 1.1)

DISRESPECTED
'How now, you secret, black, and midnight hags!' (Macbeth 4.1)

KING DUNCAN

WHO IS HE?
- A kind-hearted & well-respected king who rewards Macbeth's service & bravery with a new title, 'Thane of Cawdor.'
- He trusts Macbeth & his wife and goes to their home, where he is murdered by them in his sleep.
- His kingship is a bold contrast to that of Macbeth.

HOW HE CHANGES
There is no change, as Duncan dies.

ADMIRED BY ALL
'The king-becoming graces...Devotion, patience, courage, fortitude.' (Malcolm 4.3)

FAIR IN HIS LEADERSHIP
'Duncan/Hath borne his faculties so meek, hath been/So clear in his great office, that his virtues/Will plead like angels...' (Macbeth 1.7)

KINGSHIP v TYRANNY
- The example Duncan shows of good kingship and also what Malcolm 'may be', present a good contrast to the tyrannical king Macbeth becomes.

TRUSTING
'A most sainted King'
'This castle hath a pleasant seat; the air nimbly and sweet recommends itself unto our gentle senses.' (Duncan 1.6)

HAS BEEN FOOLED BEFORE
'He was a gentleman on whom I built/An absolute trust.' (About the Thane of Cawdor — Duncan 1.4)

HIS HEIR... MALCOLM
- Duncan's eldest son & heir to the throne.
- He takes cover before making a carefully planned challenge to Macbeth.

HOW HE CHANGES
Once his father dies, Malcolm shows signs of being an honourable king.

WEAK?
'the king's two sons,/Are stol'n away and fled; which puts suspicion of the deed.' (Macduff 2.4)

...OR WISE?
'Macbeth is ripe for the shaking.'
'Be this your whetstone of your sword: let grief Convert to anger; blunt not the heart, enrage it.' (Malcolm 4.3 to Macduff)

BANQUO

TEMPTED BY PREDICTIONS
'May they not be my oracles as well?, / And set me up in hope.' (Banquo 3.1)

TRIES TO WARN MACBETH
'...oftentimes, to win us to our harm, / The instruments of darkness tell us truths, Win us with honest trifles...' (Banquo 1.3)

DOESN'T LET AMBITION LEAD HIM ASTRAY
'...merciful powers, / Restrain in me the cursed thoughts...' (Banquo 2.1)

WILLING TO DIE FOR HIS SON
'O treachery! Fly, good Fleance, fly, fly, fly!' (Banquo 3.3)

A BETTER MAN
'Lesser than Macbeth, and greater.' (Witches 1.3)

BRAVE/WISE
'He hath a wisdom that does guide his valour.' (Macbeth 3.1)

WARY OF EVIL
'What, can the devil speak true?' (Banquo 1.3)

WHO IS HE?
- A loyal soldier, who in contrast with Macbeth, resists the witches' prophesies.
- Despite his suspicions, he doesn't act to stop Macbeth.
- Macbeth has him murdered & he later appears sitting on Macbeth's throne.

HOW HE CHANGES
He remains loyal to Macbeth, but in death (as a ghost), he comes back to torment him.

LOYAL
'My bosom franchised and allegiance clear.' (Banquo 2.1)

PERCEPTIVE
'Noble Banquo'
'Look, how our partner's rapt.' (Banquo 1.3)

SUSPICIOUS WITHOUT ACTION
'Thou hast it now...' As the weïrd women promised, and, I fear, / thou play'dst most foully for't.' (Banquo 3.1)

QUESTIONING
'...what are these So wither'd and so wild in their attire, / That look not like th'inhabitants of the earth?' (Banquo 1.3)

MACDUFF

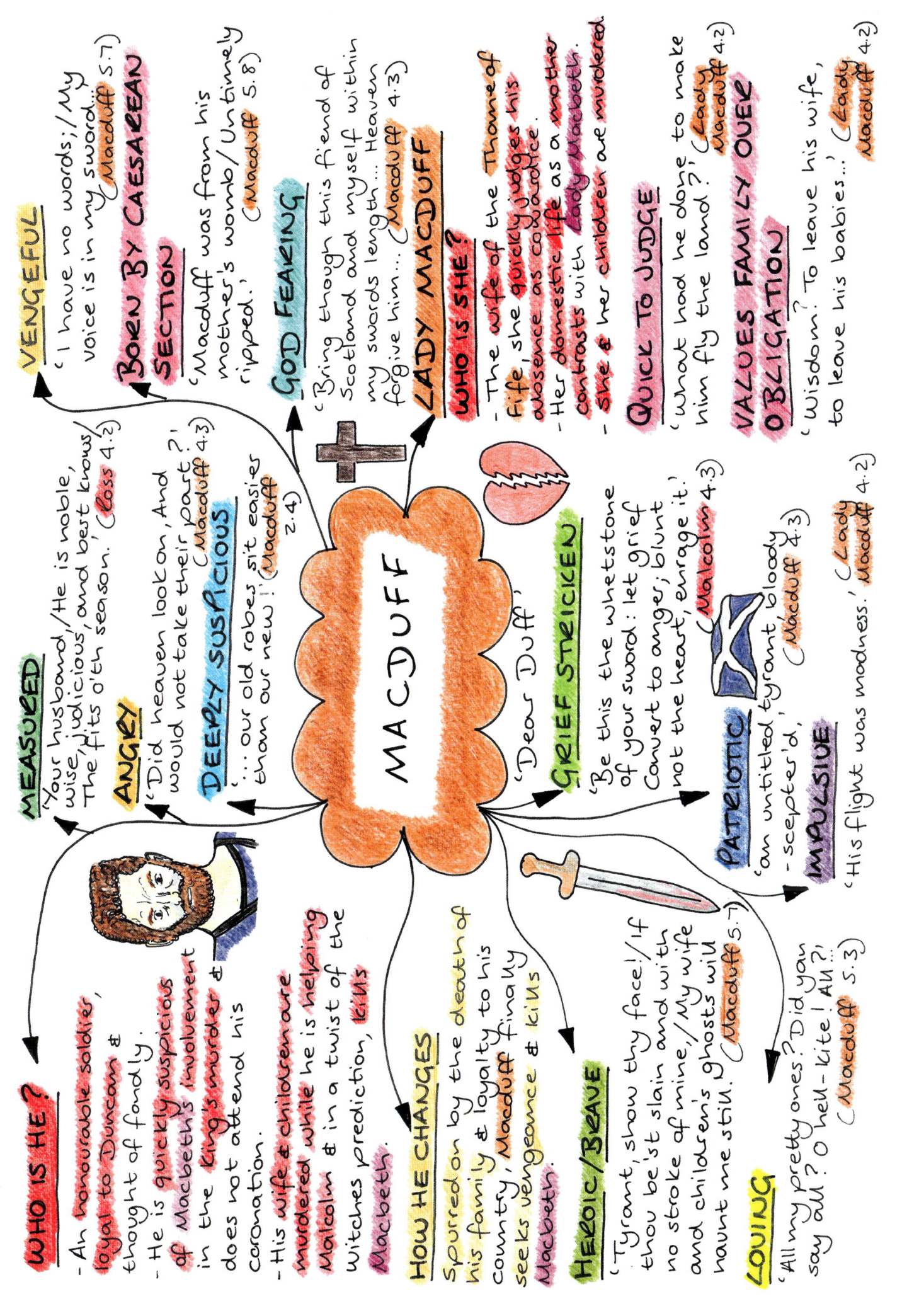

WHO IS HE?
- An honourable soldier, loyal to Duncan & thought of fondly.
- He is quickly suspicious of Macbeth's involvement in the King's murder & does not attend his coronation.
- His wife & children are murdered while he is helping Malcolm & in a twist of the witches prediction, kills Macbeth.

MEASURED
'Your husband/ He is noble, wise, judicious, and best knows/ The fits o'th' season.' (Ross 4.2)

ANGRY
'Did heaven look on, And would not take their part?' (Macduff 4.3)

DEEPLY SUSPICIOUS
'...our old robes sit easier than our new.' (Macduff 2.4)

VENGEFUL
'I have no words;/ My voice is in my sword.' (Macduff 5.7)

BORN BY CAESAREAN SECTION
'Macduff was from his mother's womb/ Untimely ripped.' (Macduff 5.8)

GOD FEARING
'Bring thou this fiend of Scotland and myself within my sword's length... Heaven forgive him...' (Macduff 4.3)

LADY MACDUFF

WHO IS SHE?
- The wife of the Thane of Fife, she quickly judges his absence as cowardice.
- Her domestic life as a mother contrasts with Lady Macbeth
- She & her children are murdered.

QUICK TO JUDGE
'What had he done to make him fly the land?' (Lady Macduff 4.2)

VALUES FAMILY OBLIGATION
'Wisdom? To leave his wife, to leave his babies...' (Lady Macduff 4.2)

HOW HE CHANGES
Spurred on by the death of his family & loyalty to his country, Macduff finally seeks vengeance & kills Macbeth.

HEROIC/BRAVE
'Tyrant, show thy face!/ If thou be'st slain and with no stroke of mine,/ My wife and children's ghosts will haunt me still.' (Macduff 5.7)

LOVING
'All my pretty ones? Did you say all? O hell-kite! All?' (Macduff 5.3)

GRIEF STRICKEN
'Be this the whetstone of your sword: let grief Convert to anger; blunt not the heart, enrage it.' (Malcolm 4.3)

'Dear Duff' (Lady Macduff 4.2)

PATRIOTIC
'an untitled tyrant bloody -scepter'd,' (Macduff 4.3)

IMPULSIVE
'His flight was madness.' (Lady Macduff 4.2)

Overview of Themes

THE SUPERNATURAL
- Witchcraft, spells & prophesies, a murdered Banquo appearing as a ghost, a vision of a dagger calling Macbeth to action & his wife calling on evil spirits to make her cruel.
- Macbeth is the most supernaturally charged of Shakespeare's plays.

APPEARANCE & REALITY
- The Macbeths appear to be loyal subjects while plotting murder. Both have strange visions (dagger, ghost/bloody hands), which may be real or imagined & honourable men (Macduff/Malcolm) are judged cowards. Shakespeare toys with the idea that everything is not always as it seems.

GUILT & REGRET
- Both Macbeth's struggle with guilt & regret at different points, Macbeth earlier on & Lady Macbeth later.
- Shakespeare looks at how guilt impacts our actions & our mental health.

GOOD & EVIL
- Shakespeare considers whether people are innately good or evil, or whether they switch. ("Fair is foul, foul is fair"). He explores the battle between the supernatural worlds of Heaven & Hell and how a person lives a Godly & ordered life.

KINGSHIP - LOYALTY & BETRAYAL
- A thane is executed for treason & while Macbeth & his wife horrifically betray their king/friends, other characters (Banquo & Macduff) present the opposite - loyalty to the end!

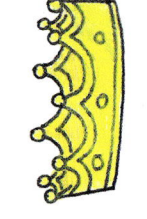

AMBITION & POWER
- The Witches' prophesy plants a seed of ambition for the crown in the hearts & minds of a previously good man & his wife.
- Through Macbeth's fatal flaw, Shakespeare examines how ruthless ambition & the desire for power & status can destroy everything!

MASCULINE & FEMININE
- Shakespeare explores what it means to be a man & a woman and how masculine & feminine traits relate to cruelty, bravery, gentleness & action, particularly through the Macbeths & the Macduffs.

FEAR & BRAVERY
- Macbeth is rewarded for his bravery in battle, but fears the consequences of murderous actions for the crown.
- Shakespeare asks what makes someone brave & can fear be good?

LIFE & DEATH
- With at least 8 deaths, Macbeth is Shakespeare's goriest play. Shakespeare considers noble & shameful deaths & what happens in death.

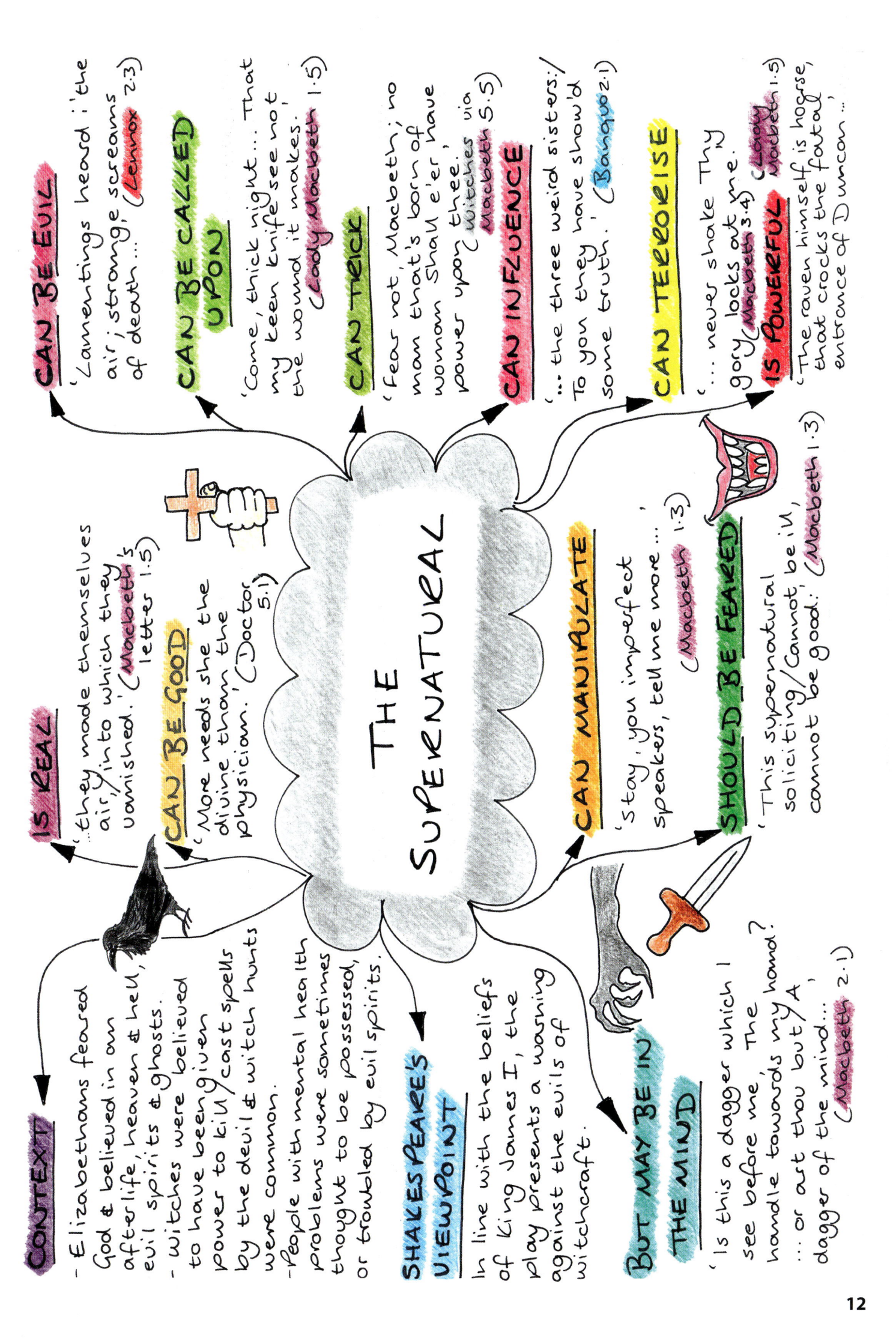

THE SUPERNATURAL

CAN BE EVIL
'Lamentings heard i' the air; strange screams of death...' (Lennox 2.3)

CAN BE CALLED UPON
'Come, thick night... that my keen knife see not the wound it makes.' (Lady Macbeth 1.5)

CAN TRICK
'Fear not, Macbeth; no man that's born of woman Shall e'er have power upon thee.' (Witches via Macbeth 5.5)

CAN INFLUENCE
'...the three weird sisters/ To you they have showed some truth.' (Banquo 2.1)

CAN TERRORISE
'...never shake Thy gory locks at me.' (Macbeth 3.4)

IS POWERFUL
'The raven himself is hoarse, that croaks the fatal entrance of Duncan.' (Lady Macbeth 1.5)

IS REAL
'...they made themselves air, into which they vanished.' (Macbeth's letter 1.5)

CAN BE GOOD
'More needs she the divine than the physician.' (Doctor 5.1)

CAN MANIPULATE
'Stay, you imperfect speakers, tell me more...' (Macbeth 1.3)

SHOULD BE FEARED
'This supernatural soliciting/ Cannot be ill, cannot be good.' (Macbeth 1.3)

CONTEXT
- Elizabethans feared God & believed in an afterlife, heaven & hell, evil spirits & ghosts.
- Witches were believed to have been given power to kill/cast spells by the devil & witch hunts were common.
- People with mental health problems were sometimes thought to be possessed, or troubled by evil spirits.

SHAKESPEARE'S VIEWPOINT
In line with the beliefs of King James I, the play presents a warning against the evils of witchcraft.

BUT MAY BE IN THE MIND
'Is this a dagger which I see before me, The handle towards my hand?/ ...or art thou but/ A dagger of the mind...' (Macbeth 2.1)

AMBITION & POWER

CONTEXT
- In Shakespeare's time, personal ambition was not considered a good quality.
- But society was hierarchical with power & status evident in <u>all</u> aspects of life.

SHAKESPEARE'S VIEWPOINT
Some ambition is good, but not for personal gain or at any cost. It can lead to tyranny, which is bad not just for the individual, but for those around them. A man who acts on his ambitions will most likely pay a heavy price for it. (FATAL FLAW)

AMBITION...

IS NATURAL
'Do you not hope your children shall be kings...?' (Banquo 1.3)

IS EVIL
'Stars, hide your fires,/Let not light see my black and deep desires...' (Macbeth 1.4)

IS SELFISH
'...thou wouldst be great,/Art not without ambition but without/The illness should attend it.' (Lady Macbeth 1.5)

IS RUTHLESS
'...I'll gild the faces of the grooms withal, For it must seem their guilt.' (Lady Macbeth 2.2)

REQUIRES DETERMINATION
'that is a step/On which I must fall down, or else o'erleap,/For in my way it lies.' (Macbeth 1.4)

CAN DESTROY YOU
- Both Macbeths die from their own ambitious desires.

POWER...

IS GOD-GIVEN
'Duncan/Hath borne his faculties so meek, hath been/So clear in his great office, that his virtues/Will plead like angels.' (Macbeth 1.7)

IS DESIRABLE
'[Aside] Two truths are told,/As happy prologues to the swelling act/Of the imperial theme.' (Macbeth 1.3)

IS INTOXICATING
'...burned in desire/to question them further.' (Macbeth 1.5)

IS PREDESTINED
'...fate and metaphysical aid doth seem/To have thee crown'd withal.' (Lady Macbeth 1.5)

SHOULD BE IN GOOD HANDS
'The king-becoming graces-/As justice, verity, temp'rance,...' (Macduff 4.3)

MASCULINE & FEMININE

MEN SHOULD BE...

BRAVE
'Let's briefly put on manly readiness,/And meet i' the hall together.' (Macbeth 2.3)

TOUGH
'Dispute it like a man.' (Malcolm 4.3)
'I must also feel it as a man.' (Macduff 4.3)

BOLD
'When you durst do it, then you are a man.' (Lady Macbeth 1.7)

READY FOR ACTION
'Prithee, peace;/I dare do all that may become a man;/Who dares do more is none.' (Macbeth 1.7)

WOMEN SHOULD BE...

BUT IN REALITY... FEEL EMOTION
'All my pretty ones? Did you say all? O hell-kite! All?' (Macduff 4.3)

FEEL FEAR
'To leave his wife, to leave his babes.' (Lady Macduff 4.2)

NURTURING
'I have given suck, and know/How tender 'tis to love the babe that milks me.' (Lady Macbeth 1.7)

REQUIRE SUPERNATURAL HELP
'Come to my woman's breasts,/And take my milk for gall, you murdering ministers.' (Lady Macbeth 1.5)

BUT IN REALITY... ARE IN CONTROL
'Leave all the rest to me.' (Lady Macbeth 1.5)

AND THEIR ATTEMPTS TO TAKE ON MANLY TRAITS...

ARE EVIL
'I would, while it was smiling in my face,/Have plucked my nipple from his boneless gums,/And dashed the brains out.' (Lady Macbeth 1.7)

CONTEXT
- Women in the 1600s were expected to have domestic & nurturing roles, but...
- Queen Elizabeth I claimed to have 'the heart of a man' and '...be not afraid of anything.' She was said to have a 'masculine spirit.'
- Queen Elizabeth I had King James I's mother (Mary Queen of Scots) killed.

SHAKESPEARE'S VIEWPOINT
Shakespeare uses two very different couples, the Macbeths & Macduffs to explore gender roles.

Some of Shakespeare's love sonnets are addressed to men. Could this be why the idea of masculine/feminine interested him?

APPEARANCE & REALITY

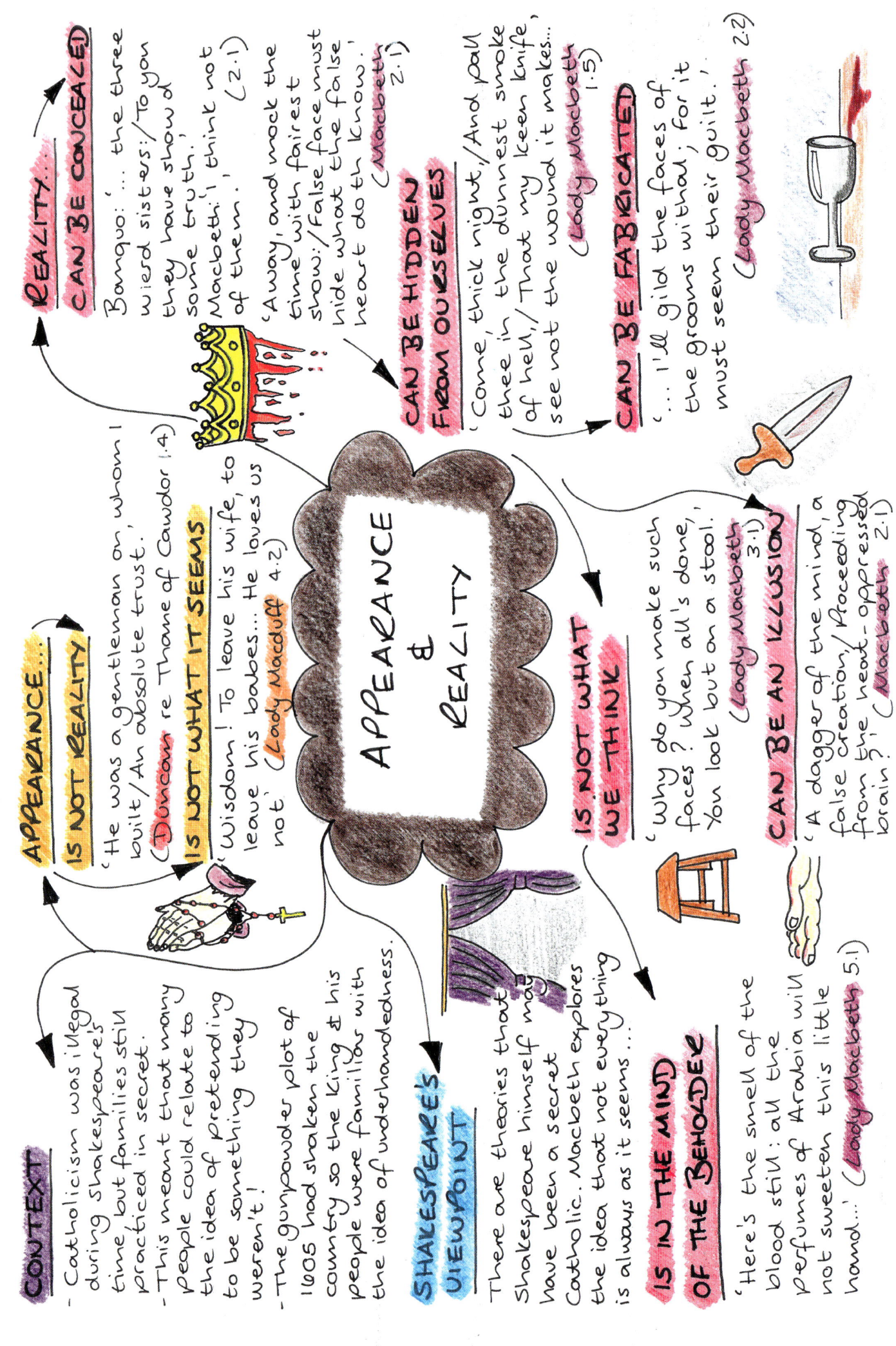

REALITY...

CAN BE CONCEALED
Banquo: '... the three wierd sisters:/To you they have show of some truth.' Macbeth: 'I think not of them.' (2.1)

'Away, and mock the time with fairest show:/False face must hide what the false heart doth know.' (Macbeth 2.1)

CAN BE HIDDEN FROM OURSELVES
'Come, thick night,/And pall thee in the dunnest smoke of hell,/That my keen knife see not the wound it makes...' (Lady Macbeth 1.5)

CAN BE FABRICATED
'...I'll gild the faces of the grooms withal; for it must seem their guilt.' (Lady Macbeth 2.2)

APPEARANCE...

IS NOT REALITY
'He was a gentleman on whom I built/An absolute trust.' (Duncan re Thane of Cawdor 1.4)

IS NOT WHAT IT SEEMS
'Wisdom! To leave his wife, to leave his babes... He loves us not.' (Lady Macduff 4.2)

IS NOT WHAT WE THINK
'Why do you make such faces? When all's done, You look but on a stool.' (Lady Macbeth 3.1)

CAN BE AN ILLUSION
'A dagger of the mind, a false creation, proceeding from the heat-oppressed brain?' (Macbeth 2.1)

IS IN THE MIND OF THE BEHOLDER
'Here's the smell of the blood still; all the perfumes of Arabia will not sweeten this little hand...' (Lady Macbeth 5.1)

CONTEXT
- Catholicism was illegal during Shakespeare's time but families still practiced in secret.
- This meant that many people could relate to the idea of pretending to be something they weren't!
- The gunpowder plot of 1605 had shaken the country so the King & his people were familiar with the idea of underhandedness.

SHAKESPEARE'S VIEWPOINT
There are theories that Shakespeare himself may have been a secret Catholic. Macbeth explores the idea that not everything is always as it seems...

GUILT & REGRET

GUILT & REGRET...

HAUNTS YOU
'Bloody instructions, which, being taught, return/To plague the inventor.' (Macbeth 1.7)

STEALS PEACE
'Whence is that knocking? How is't with me, when every noise appalls me?' (Macbeth 2.2)

STEALS HAPPINESS
'Naught's had, all's spent,/Where our desire is got without content.' (Lady Macbeth 3.2)

CAUSES MISERY
'Better be with the dead… Than on the torture of the mind to lie in restless ecstasy.' (Macbeth 3.2)

LASTS FOREVER
'Ere we will eat our meal in fear and sleep/In the affliction of these terrible dreams/That shake us nightly.' (Macbeth 3.2)

BREAKS THE RELATIONSHIP WITH GOD
'I could not say "Amen,"/When they did say "God bless us."' (Macbeth 2.2)

BUT... IS POINTLESS
'Things without all remedy/Should be without regard:/What's done is done.' (Lady Macbeth 3.2)

CAN BE IGNORED
'Make thick my blood,/Stop up the access and passage to remorse,/That no compunctious visitings of nature/Shake my fell purpose.' (Lady Macbeth 1.5)

'These deeds must not be thought/After these ways; so, it will make us mad.' (Lady Macbeth 2.2)

CONTEXT
- Christianity taught that true repentance leads to forgiveness & peace of mind.
- Mental health wasn't treated medically, so anxiety & delusions were seen as spiritual problems that could only be made right with God's help.

SHAKESPEARE'S VIEWPOINT
Shakespeare appears to have personal experience of the power of guilt to eat away at the human mind.

We can speculate that perhaps like most of us, Shakespeare held some regrets… perhaps about his son's death, or living away in London.

16

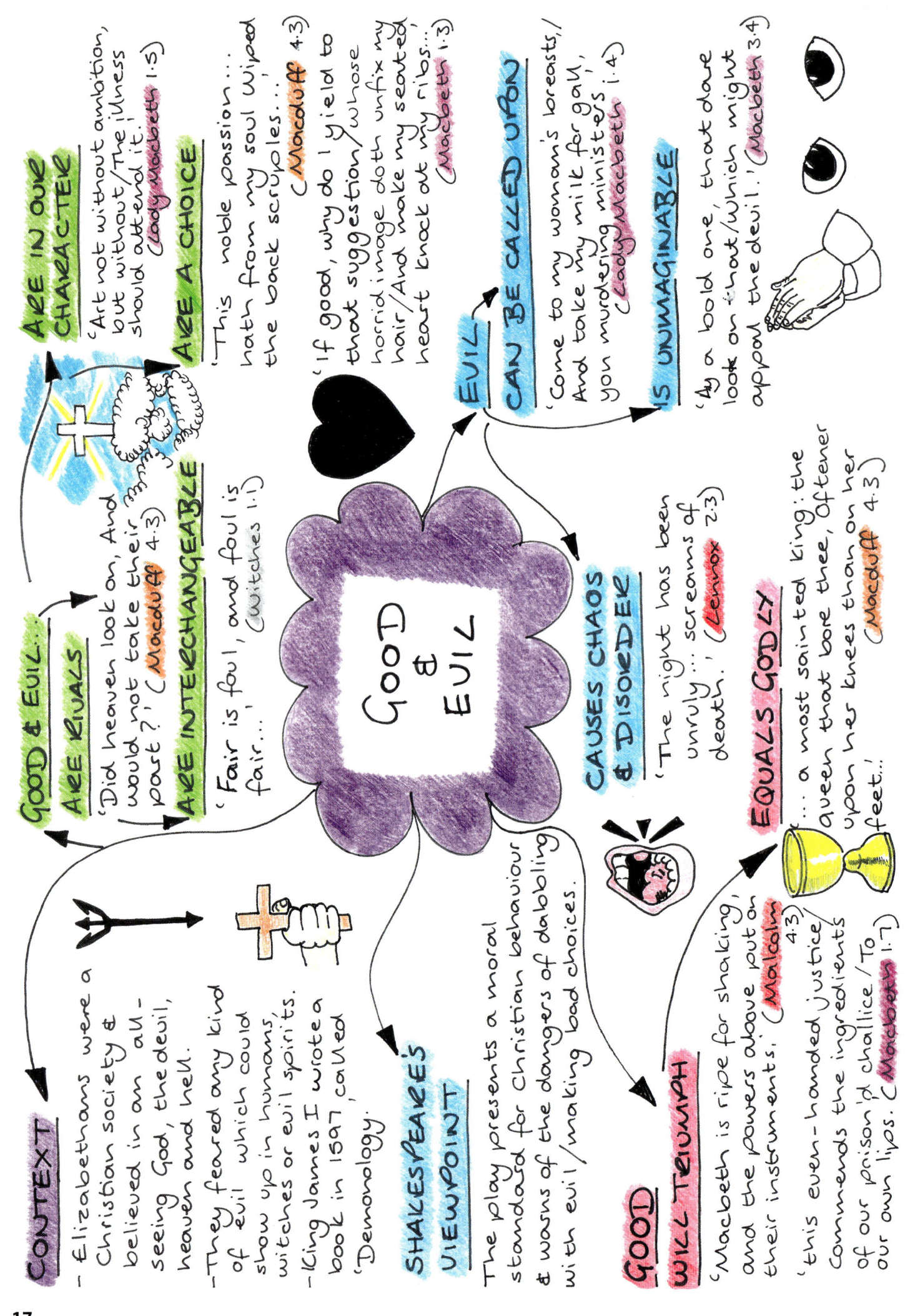

GOOD & EVIL

CONTEXT
- Elizabethans were a Christian society & believed in an all-seeing God, the devil, heaven and hell.
- They feared any kind of evil which could show up in humans, witches or evil spirits.
- King James I wrote a book in 1597 called 'Demonology'.

SHAKESPEARE'S VIEWPOINT
The play presents a moral standard for Christian behaviour & warns of the dangers of dabbling with evil / making bad choices.

GOOD & EVIL...

ARE IN OUR CHARACTER
'Art not without ambition, but without the illness should attend it.' (Lady Macbeth 1.5)

ARE A CHOICE
'This noble passion... hath from my soul wiped the back scruples...' (Macduff 4.3)

'If good, why do I yield to that suggestion/whose horrid image doth unfix my hair/And make my seated heart knock at my ribs...' (Macbeth 1.3)

ARE EQUALS
'Did heaven look on, And would not take their part?' (Macduff 4.3)

ARE INTERCHANGEABLE
'Fair is foul, and foul is fair...' (Witches 1.1)

EVIL

CAN BE CALLED UPON
'Come to my woman's breasts, / And take my milk for gall, you murdering ministers' (Lady Macbeth 1.4)

IS UNIMAGINABLE
'Ay a bold one that dare look on that/which might appal the devil.' (Macbeth 3.4)

CAUSES CHAOS & DISORDER
'The night has been unruly... screams of death.' (Lennox 2.3)

GOOD

EQUALS GODLY
'...a most sainted king: the queen that bore thee, Oftener upon her knees than on her feet...' (Macduff 4.3)

WILL TRIUMPH
'Macbeth is ripe for shaking, and the powers above put on their instruments.' (Malcolm 4.3)

'this even-handed justice commends the ingredients of our prison'd chalice / To our own lips.' (Macbeth 1.7)

FEAR & BRAVERY

IS WEAK
'His flight was madness: when our actions do not, Our fears do make us traitors.' (Lady Macduff about Macduff 4.2)

IS DESPICABLE
'Go prick thy face, and over-red thy fear, Thou lily-liver'd boy.' (Macbeth 5.3)

IS CHILDISH
''Tis the eye of childhood/That fears a painted devil.' (Lady Macbeth 2.2)

SHOWS GUILT
'What had he done, to make him fly the land?' (Lady Macduff about her husband 4.2)

CAN BE WISE
'You know not whether it was his wisdom or his fear.' (Ross to Lady Macduff 4.2)

IS TO BE ADMIRED
'The mind I sway by, and the heart I bear/Shall never sag with doubt nor shake with fear.' (Macbeth 5.3)

FEAR...

IS COWARDLY
'Wisdom! to leave his wife, to leave his babes...' (Lady Macduff 4.2)

CAN SAVE
'Fly, good Fleance, fly, fly, fly!' (Banquo 3.3)

BRAVERY...

CAN BE FOOLISH
'Till Birnam wood remove to Dunsinane, I cannot taint with fear.' (Macbeth 5.3)

IS A CHOICE
'Infirm of purpose!/Give me the daggers: the sleeping and the dead/Are but as pictures.' (Lady Macbeth 2.2)

CONTEXT
- Cowardice was regarded with contempt & bravery revered.
- The play holds bravery & risking your life for King & country/friend/son in the highest esteem.

BRAVERY

FEAR

SHAKESPEARE'S VIEWPOINT
Shakespeare seems to admire bravery and sees cowardice as shameful. James I was considered quite a weak King, so it could have been written to massage his ego, or even have a little dig.

IS MASCULINE
'Dispute it like a man.' (Malcolm in face of Macduff's grief 4.3)

'Let's briefly put on manly readiness,/And meet i' the hall together.' (Macbeth 2.3)

KINGSHIP, LOYALTY & BETRAYAL

A KING...

CAN BE WRONGLY CROWNED
'Fit to govern?/No, not to live...With an untitled tyrant bloody-scepter'd.' (Malcolm 4.3)

IS DIVINELY CHOSEN
'God save the king!' (Ross 1.2)

IS HONOURABLE
'The king-becoming graces...Devotion, patience, courage, fortitude...' (Malcolm 4.3)

BETRAYAL IS...

DISHONOURABLE
'O, treachery! Fly, good Fleance...fly!' (Banquo 3.3)

A CHOICE
'He's here in double trust;/First, as I am his kinsman and his subject,/Strong both against the deed; then, as his host,/Who should against his murderer shut the door,/Not bear the knife myself.' (Macbeth 1.7)

PUNISHABLE BY DEATH
'he confess'd his treasons... nothing in his life/Became him like the leaving it.' (Malcolm re Thane of Cawdor 1.4)

REQUIRES AVENGING
'Bring thou this fiend of Scotland and myself; within my sword's length set him...' (Macduff 4.3)

CAN BE ABUSED
'What cannot you and I perform upon/The unguarded Duncan?' (Lady Macbeth 1.7)

LOYALTY...

CAN BE FAKED
'There's daggers in men's smiles.' (Donalbain 2.3)

CAN BE QUESTIONED
'the king's two sons/Are stol'n away and fled, which puts upon them/Suspicion of the deed.' (Macduff 2.4)

REVENGE...

CAN HEAL
'Let's make us medicines of our great revenge,/To cure this deadly grief.' (Malcolm 4.3)

CAN EMPOWER
'Be this the whetstone of your sword...blunt not the heart, enrage it.' (Malcolm 4.3)

CONTEXT
- Kings were believed to have been divinely chosen by God.
- Kings expected loyalty from their subjects.
- King James I was terrified of being assassinated.
- A foiled gunpowder plot & the expulsion of Catholic priests were fresh in the public's mind.

SHAKESPEARE'S VIEWPOINT
Shakespeare appears to hold kingship & loyalty in high regard. That said, he was effectively employed by James I & would have ensured the play's content kept him happy.

LIFE & DEATH

LIFE...

IS INSIGNIFICANT
'Life's but a walking shadow, a poor player/ That struts and frets his hour upon the stage...' (Macbeth 5.5)

IS FLEETING
'Out out brief candle!' (Macbeth 5.5)

IS MEANINGLESS
'It is a tale/ Told by an idiot, full of sound and fury/ Signifying nothing.' (Macbeth 5.5)

DEATH...

IS BRUTAL
'O horror, horror, horror! Tongue nor heart/ Cannot conceive nor name thee!' (Macduff at Duncan's death 2.3)

CAN BRING HONOUR
'nothing in his life/ Became him like the leaving it;' (Malcolm re Thane of Cawdor 1.4)

IS PREDESTINED
'The raven himself is hoarse That croaks the fatal entrance of Duncan...' (Lady Macbeth 1.5)

CAUSES SORROW
'All my pretty ones? Did you say all? O hell-kite!' (Macduff 4.3)

BRINGS PEACE
'Heaven rest them now!' Duncan is in his grave; After life's fitful fever he sleeps well;' (Macbeth 3.2)

CONTEXT
- Life expectancy was short (average 30 years). Babies & mothers died during childbirth. Half of all children died before their 15th birthday.
- People were painfully aware of the fragility of life & the hope of an afterlife made this bearable.

SHAKESPEARE'S VIEWPOINT
Shakespeare's only son Hamnet died aged 11. Shakespeare wrote many lines about the fleeting nature of life, the pain of losing loved ones & the peace of the afterlife.

GRIEF...

IS NECESSARY
'I must feel it as a man;' (Macduff 4.3)

Form & Structure

Use of Dramatic Devices

Soliloquy
- To reveal a character's internal state of mind. Macbeth has 7 at key moments (1.3, 1.7, 2.1, 3.1, 4.1, 5.1, 5.5).

Asides
- Also reveal what a character is thinking.
- In 1.3, Macbeth has 5.

Prose & Verse
- Shakespeare generally writes in **Iambic Pentameter** (see page 25). This is especially true for significant moments.

Rhyming Couplets
- (See page 26). Rhyming couplets are used at the end of speeches/conversation for emphasis.

Prose
- Is used for low status characters & to show Lady Macbeth's unravelling whilst sleepwalking. (See page 26)

Trochaic Tetrameter
- (See page 26), is only used for the witches to show they are other worldly.

Chronologically Told
- ... as time passes. Some major events happen offstage e.g. Duncan's murder, Macbeth being crowned, Lady Macbeth's suicide.

5 Act Structure
Held together by a CROWN.

ACT I
- Macbeth's want (the CROWN) is ignited by the witches' predictions.

ACT II
- Macbeth kills the king, the princes flee & Macbeth is CROWNED king.

ACT III
- Fears of the CROWN being taken lead to Macbeth having Banquo killed & facing his ghost.

ACT IV
- The witches reassure Macbeth, while Malcolm & Macduff form a plan to take back the CROWN.

ACT V
- There is a battle for the CROWN. Macduff kills Macbeth & Malcolm is CROWNED king.

IN THE EXAM

SOME HELPFUL SENTENCE STARTERS

- Shakespeare depicts/ presents/ suggests/ implies/ employs/ represents/ creates a sense of....
- The character of '...' is shown as / presented as....
- The word '...' shows us/ creates a sense of/ creates a picture of....
- This alludes to/ is reminiscent of/ has echoes of/ reminds us of/ connotes...
- Similarly / likewise / furthermore.....
- Conversely....
- In contrast....

GAIN MAXIMUM MARKS

- Choose a quotation relevant to the question & point.
- Consider how the quotation reflects character/theme/context.
- Explore in detail the impact of specific words or phrases.
- Evaluate how effective the author's choice of language is.

ANSWER THE QUESTION

- Read & understand what is being asked.
- Plan your answer.
- Refer to 5-6 quotes.
- Zoom in/focus in on key language/words.
- Include Shakespeare's/your viewpoint as well as context.

DON'T FORGET...

- Use the best vocabulary you can.
- Use single quotation marks, unless the quote uses "speech."
- Refer to other key moments from the play (if relevant).
- Check spelling & grammar.

EXAMPLES OF SPECIFIC LANGUAGE/LITERARY DEVICES

ACT – part of a play, defined by elements such as rising action, climax and resolution.

ADJECTIVE – a word describing a noun. eg- 'the curtain'd sleep', 'vaulting ambition', 'direst cruelty.'

ALLITERATION – the reoccurrence of the same letter or sound in adjacent or close words. eg- 'bloody business'.

ALLUSION – an indirect reference to a historical person or event. eg- 'witchcraft celebrates Pale Hecate's offerings.'

ANTITHESIS – eg- the direct opposite. eg- 'heaven and hell', 'foul and fair.'

ASIDE – A character speaks an inner thought to himself (and the audience). eg- 'MACBETH [Aside] Two truths are told, As happy prologues to the swelling act.'

BLANK VERSE – poetry written in unrhymed, metered lines, almost always iambic pentameter.

CATALYST – an event which triggers a reaction and sets a chain of events in motion. eg- the witches' predictions.

CONTRAST – a comparison of difference. eg- Banquo & Macbeth's different reactions to the predictions.

DRAMATIC IRONY – when the reader knows something a character doesn't. eg- the Macbeths welcoming Duncan after plotting his murder.

DIRECT ADDRESS TO OBJECTS – 'Come, let me clutch thee./ I have thee not, and yet I still see thee' to dagger.

ENTRANCE – when or how a character comes onto stage.

EXIT – when or how a character leaves the stage.

ECHO – where something is repeated, or reminds us of something previously heard or seen. eg- Macbeth comments on the 'foul and fair day' after the witches incantation.

EMOTIVE LANGUAGE – words and phrases meant to evoke a strong emotional response. eg- '...while it was smiling in my face,/ Have pluck'd my nipple from his boneless gums,/ And dash'd the brains out.'

EXTRACT - a section of text.

EXPOSITION - how the writer gives us information. eg - We learn of Macbeth's success in battle before we meet him.

FATAL FLAW - the tragic pattern of the character weakness, which leads a good person onto a path of their own destruction. eg - the extreme ambition of Macbeth.

FLOWERY LANGUAGE - heavily descriptive and emotive writing. eg - 'heaven's cherubim, horsed/Upon the sightless couriers of the air,/Shall blow the horrid deed in every eye.'

FOIL - a character who contrasts with another character to highlight different qualities. eg - Macduff to Macbeth.

FORESHADOWING - a hint or warning at a future event. eg - 'why do you dress me in borrow'd robes?'

HYPERBOLE - exaggerated statements or claims not meant to be taken literally. eg - 'Will all great Neptune's ocean wash this blood clean from my hand?'

IDIOM - A group of words which come to mean something. eg - 'be-all and end-all', which after their use in Macbeth came to mean 'the most important thing'.

IAMBIC PENTAMETER - An unstressed syllable followed by a stressed syllable x 5 (da DUM...) See eg - next line

IMAGERY - visually descriptive language. eg - 'whose hor/rid im/age doth/unfix/my hair.'

JUXTAPOSITION - two things being placed close together with contrasting effect. eg - Macbeth being given his new title for loyalty to the king, while his ambition is being ignited by the witches predictions.

METAPHOR - a comparison which describes one thing as another. eg - 'I have no spur/To prick the sides of my intent.'

MONOLOGUE - a lengthy speech by one character which can be directed to another character, or spoken alone.

MOOD - the tone and atmosphere created. eg - 'Double double, toil and trouble.'

MOTIF – an image or action repeated throughout the text. eg – the use of blood to symbolise the stain of guilt.

PARADOX – a contradiction. eg – 'When the battle's lost and won.'

PATHETIC FALLACY – the way weather or other inanimate things are described to create a mood or emotion. eg – 'Fair is foul and foul is fair. Hover through the fog and filthy air.'

PERSONIFICATION – giving an object or animal human characteristics. eg – 'The raven himself is hoarse/That croaks the final entrance of Duncan.'

PROSE – ordinary writing/speech usually used for common people by Shakespeare.

PROTAGONIST – the central character. eg – Macbeth.

REPETITION – the repeating of words or phrases for emphasis. eg – 'Cannot be ill, cannot be good.' The words blood/bloody are used 40 times in the play!

RHYMING COUPLET – two lines written in iambic pentameter that end in the same sound/rhyme. They are often used to sum up the end of a character's speech. eg – 'Hear it not, Duncan – for it is a knell/That summons thee to heaven or to hell.'

SIMILE – a comparison using 'as' or 'like'. eg – 'Whole as the marble, founded as the rock.'

SENSORY DESCRIPTION – language that stimulates the senses. eg – 'Come thick night,/And pall thee in the dunnest smoke of hell,/That my keen knife see not the wound it makes.'

SOLILOQUY – a longer speech or monologue spoken by one character to themself, revealing inner thoughts to the audience.

SYNONYMS – long lists of adjectives and verbs, or examples of behaviour to emphasise a trait. eg – 'the king-becoming graces, As justice, verity, temperance, stableness...'

SYMBOLISM – an image with a deeper, often recognisable meaning. eg – the dagger Macbeth sees points blame & tells him what he should do.

TRAGEDY – a play where a tragic hero (often with a fatal flaw) makes poor choices, destroying himself & others.

TROCHAIC TETRAMETER – the opposite of iambic pentameter; a stressed syllable followed by an unstressed syllable (Dum-da...) x5 eg – Double/double/toil and/trouble...'

QUESTIONS TO THINK ABOUT

Character Questions

How does Shakespeare present...

- Macbeth as a powerful character?
- Macbeth as a man who is in control?
- Macbeth's state of mind?
- Macbeth as a man who struggles with a guilty conscience?
- Macbeth's reaction to the witches?
- Macbeth as a troubled character?
- Lady Macbeth as an ambitious woman with influence over her husband?
- Lady Macbeth as a dangerous character?
- The attitudes of Macbeth and Banquo towards the supernatural?

How does...

- Macbeth change during the course of the play?
- Shakespeare portray the relationship between Macbeth and Lady Macbeth?
- Shakespeare compare the Macduffs with the Macbeths?

Theme Questions

How does Shakespeare present...

- Kingship?
- Loyalty / betrayal?
- Leadership?
- Ambition?
- Fear & bravery?
- Guilt & regret?
- Life & death?
- Appearance & reality?
- Fate & free will?
- Good & evil?
- The witches as evil?
- Witchcraft & the supernatural?
- Hallucinations
- The disruption of nature?
- Chaos & disorder?
- Women?
- Masculinity?
- Inner conflict / guilt?

NOTES